Trains Across the Country

by Carol Koeller
Illustrated by Peter Smith

Glenview, Illinois • Boston, Massachusetts • Chandler, Arizona
Upper Saddle River, New Jersey

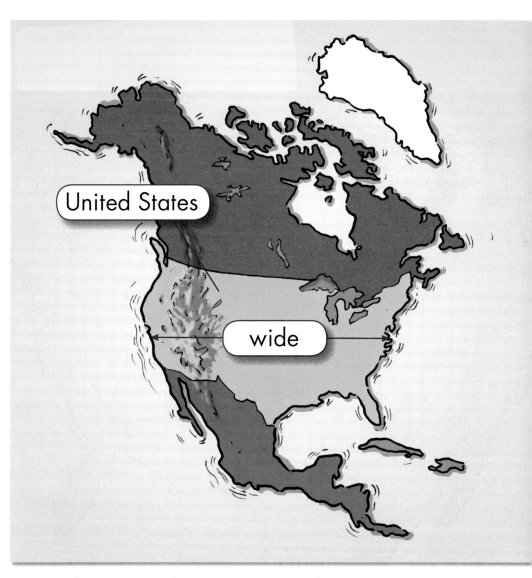

United States

wide

The United States is wide.
Long ago, it was hard to travel.
Trains did not go across the country.

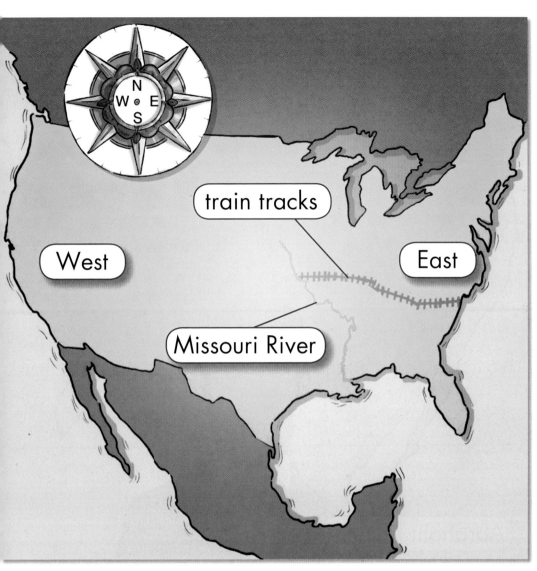

train tracks

West

East

Missouri River

In 1862, train tracks stopped at the
Missouri River.
No tracks went from east to west.
People went west on horses.
People also traveled in wagons.

Abraham Lincoln

People wanted to travel west.
Abraham Lincoln wanted to help.
He wanted to make train tracks
longer.

workers

train tracks

Two groups of workers started
building tracks.
One group started at the
Missouri River.
One group started in California.

workers

Workers came from many countries.
It was hard work.
They worked for many years.

In 1869, the two groups of
workers met.
The train tracks were ready!
Now people could travel across the
country.

train

The first trains were very slow.
A trip from east to west took
many weeks.
Today, trains are fast.
They can go across the country
in three days.